IMAGES OF ENGLAND

DIDCOT
REVISITED

IMAGES OF ENGLAND

DIDCOT
REVISITED

KEN CAULKETT

The
History
Press

Frontispiece: Dinner may be a little late today. Mr Ern Gardener shares a joke with the family.

First published in 2006 by Tempus Publishing

Reprinted in 2011 by
The History Press
The Mill, Brimscombe Port,
Stroud, Gloucestershire, GL5 2QG
www.thehistorypress.co.uk

Reprinted 2013

British Library Cataloguing in Publication Data.
A catalogue record for this book is available from the British Library.

ISBN 978 0 7524 3970 9

Typesetting and origination by
Tempus Publishing Limited.
Printed in Great Britain.

Contents

Acknowledgements

This book is dedicated to all of our local photographers, both amateurs and professionals; without their skill and devotion this book could not have been printed. Thanks must also go to: Mr David Wharton for his brilliant work on his computer where he brought photos back to life from obscurity; Miss Sharon Wharton for all her hard work typing, especially with my constant changes of mind; and Mr Chris Buratta for his article in the *Didcot Herald* which enabled me to receive many photos. I would also like to thank all the people who entrusted me with their photographs. Lastly, thanks are due to our local historian Mr Brian F. Lingham for the introduction to this book.

Introduction

Ken Caulkett is to be congratulated on producing another book of photographs of Didcot people. His first was a great success, and this second volume will, no doubt, be equally successful. Although, primarily, this is a book of personal photographs – what Ken calls a 'family photo album' – to me it's more than that, for many of the photographs are very evocative, a reminder of Didcot's past and its cultural history.

A good example is the picture of the dancing display at the old Garrison Theatre, taken in the early 1950s. The Garrison Theatre, sited formerly at the Didcot army barracks, was erected in 1940-41. It was a popular venue for the people of Didcot, who flocked there during the war and afterwards. The theatre burned down in the mid–1950s, but it had a brief moment of fame during the Second World War. In April 1943, as part of a fund-raising initiative for Didcot Hospital, Steve Donohue, the famous jockey, in honouring a long-standing promise to do something substantial for the fund, arranged with his friend Jack Hylton, the London impresario, to bring his new revue, Hi-de-Hi, to the Garrison Theatre.

The charity evening was a sell-out. The cast, which included Florence Desmond, Eddie Grey, Flanagan and Allen, Wilson, Keppel and Betty, as well as others, gave their services free of charge. During the interval, Flanagan and Allen, Steve Donohue and jockey Gordon Richards raised £686 by auctioning wines, spirits and other gifts. In total £1,000 was made that evening, with sixty per cent going to the hospital and forty to the Red Cross's prisoner of war fund. The money raised for the hospital meant that it was to be endowed with a maternity ward.

The photograph of the army depot police of 1927 shows how important the depot was before the war, and that a heavy police presence was needed to keep out all strangers; to that end, roads and footpaths were blocked off, at the inconvenience of many in Didcot. The first police force of 1915 were constables brought from London.

Another evocative photo is the dance in 1952, staged by the Barn Theatre Group at the Old Coronet Ballroom, to raise funds for the Barn Theatre on Park Road. The theatre was a very popular place of entertainment throughout the 1950s and '60s, but eventually fell by the wayside, presumably due to lack of support in the 1970s. It occupied a former WMCA building erected in 1940-41.

Before the era of the motor car and television, people were compelled to go from their homes for entertainment, to the new Coronet Cinema on the Broadway, to the Garrison Theatre, to the social club at the barracks, to the community centre on Station Road, or later to the Barn Theatre. Then there were dances, of which at least three were staged each week, such as those at the Coronet Ballroom. Whist Drives were also popular.

The Marlborough Club was very successful, its membership then drawn from across the social divide. Outings by coach, or special excursions by train to the seaside were equally popular, staged either by the churches, the youth clubs or the political parties. Parades were far more common than they are now, as were carnivals and gymkhanas.

Several photographs in this book portray these pastimes. Going out to a dance, to the community centre or on an outing helped the process of social cohesion, enabling people to meet others and make new friends. Unfortunately, many of these social meeting places no longer exist.

There is one interesting group of photographs: the RP at work in the Vestas at the beginning of the Second World War. They may seem quaint, even funny today, but these men were then practising in deadly earnest. The people of Didcot in 1939 and 1940 thought that they would be bombed heavily; and the local authority was expecting to have to cope with hundreds of casualties. The reason for this fear was that Didcot was, at the time, sited between the two large army and RAF depots. But their fears were groundless. The Germans didn't consider the depots a strategic target, and in fact there was only one raid, on Milton Depot in November 1940.

The Vestas, or the Parkside Estate as this area of Didcot was once known (i.e. Bowness Avenue, Tavistock Avenue, South Park Avenue and part of Queensway, formerly Parkside), figure greatly in the book. The Vestas have a chequered history: the estate of 194 houses was built in 1934 and was regarded in those years as Didcot's slum area. The houses were badly built, being cold and damp, but there was a vigorous spirit abroad in the estate. Through great pressure from tenants and the local authority, the houses were slowly improved and renovated, so much so that today's houses bear no resemblance to those of the 1940s.

Events in Edmonds Park are another feature. The park has always, especially in the past, been a centre for carnivals, other events and fairs. This was especially so during the 1930s and '40s, but nowadays it seems to be used just for fairs. Its main use today is for football and rugby. The park has a long history dating back to the 1330s, when the abbots of Cirencester received permission to convert this part of East Hagbourne into a hunting park. Though its function has changed, it was always known as the Park. In the nineteenth and early twentieth centuries, it was often used to stage fairs, and this was due to a councillor called Ernest Edmonds who worked hard to acquire the land for Didcot from its owners, Allens of Down Farm. The local authority finally bought the land in 1934. Edmonds, a railway engine driver, was killed in a dreadful accident in March 1935, and in his memory it was named Edmonds Park.

These are just a few examples of the wealth of material contained in this book, and I heartily recommend it to those thinking of buying a copy.

Brian Ling
Didcot, 2006

one

People at Work, Work Functions, The Park

Staff of the Co-op in the 1950s. The shop on the Broadway next to the cinema was originally called the Coronet Ballroom. Front row from left to right: Beryl Cox, Betty Ireson, Gill Ireson, -?-, Jill Little, ? Haines, -?-, -?-. Middle, second row: Rosemary Hare, Sylvia Escot (second from right), Geraldine Wadley (fourth from right).

Didcot Market, 1950. In the background can be seen a row of cottages, which were known as Mount Pleasant but commonly called the 'Barracks'.

Harvey Bradfield Toyer Netball Team, 1960. From left to right: Jean Williams, Pam Buckle, -?-, Alison Burfit, Joan Bued (?), Sheila Barnes, Yvonne Beard.

Ladies Typing Pool, Didcot Depot, 1946-48. Front row, from left to right: Marion Lancaster, -?-, -?-, Betty Moody, Hilda Longshaw, Jean Harris, Joyce Middlehurst. Second row: Barbara Moon, Florrie Bowes, Olwen Cuff, Mrs Wilson, Miss Kennedy, Edna Mason, Edna Tibble, Joyce Sandford, Muriel Reeves, -?-. Third row: Mary Case, Beryl Carter, Eileen Nunn, ? Smart, Kath Wigley, Pat Gallaghan, -?-, -?-, Joan Beaman, Mary Dorn, Muriel Grant. Back row: Ruth Stovin, Edna Cook, -?-, -?-, -?-, -?-, -?-, Ivy Reed, Iris Barrett, Iris Haingus, Betty Roger.

Above: Harvey Bradfield Children's Party, 1960.

A group girls enjoy the day. From left to right: Freida Essex, Violet Hill, Maggie Avery, Gwen Ovens, Sheila Essex, Pat Smith, Marge Carter.

Above: Time to call it a day at the glove factory. In the line on the left: Pat Smith (foreground), Marge Carter (rear). Middle line: Freida Essex, Violet Hill, Sheila Essex. Standing right: Barbara Lovelock.

Opposite below: The glove factory – party time. The workers, sitting on the floor, from left to right, are: Harry Amphlett, Charlie Grant, Freida Essex, Albert Beard, Pat Smith. Sitting: -?-, -?-, Miss Spokes, Mr Bolton, -?-, Maggie Avery, Violet Hill, Maggie Carter, Rosemary Keats. Standing: Barbara Lovelock, Fred Amphlett, Joyce Wootton, Doris Shepherd, Eunice Bennett, Anita Lyford, Judy Aldworth, Violet Mcloughlin, Jean Target, Gwen Ovens, Janet Vincent, -?-, -?-, Pauline Aldsworth, Stella Cummings. Rear (right side of photo): Jane Walton, Jack Amphlett, Gwen West, Tony Bolton.

Left: The Didcot St John's Brigade in the 1950s. Ron Stevenson and (top left) Robert Russel, (top right) Pauline Musson, (bottom left) Adrian Shaw and (bottom right) Stephen Gayley collect the cup.

Below: This photograph was taken by one of the lads on the line and shows Jeff from Faringdon and Graham Fry of Didcot working on the last MG car to come off the assembly line at Abingdon, on 22 October 1980. Note the empty line behind.

Opposite above: Canning factory Christmas dinner and dance, 1966. Back row, from left to right: Tommy Jepson, Gordon Purvis, Graham Fry. Front row: Sheila Jepson, Rosemary Fry, June Purvis.

Opposite below: Didcot St John Ambulance. The St John Ambulance pose for a photograph outside the old headquarters at the Junction of Hagbourne Road and Wessex Road. Seated in the centre is Ron Stevenson.

Above: Workmates: Stan Bishop, John Belton and Les Stratton all together.

Below: RAF Milton Fire Brigade in the 1950s. Ern Kent is on the right with three of his colleagues from the No. 3 maintenance unit.

Right: The ladies who ran the canning factory nursery. From left to right: Mrs Holman, Mrs Leithwait, Mrs Hayes.

Below: Gang of Didcot steel fixers, 1962. From left to right: Bob McGibbon, Don Whyte, Mick Wicks, Richard Elsley, Trevor Giles and also Bill Joslin.

Egg packing station, North Moreton, 1956. Enjoying a cuppa are: Don Whyte, Tony Thornhill, Jackie Earl, Betty Aldridge.

Cyril Moxon's fruit stall at Didcot Carnival, on the hospital field, 1935-36. Pictured are Edith Moxon, Joe Moxon (with a very young John Rowland), Cyril Moxon and Stella Rowland.

Right: Mr A.E. Rowland, Snr, delivering bread in Didcot probably in the 1920s. He began his bakery business in Didcot but then moved to Upton where it continued until 1953. His wasn't the only local bakery, as both Livings and Fulfords also served the town.

Below: Charles Alan (Sonny) Caulkett, Weymouth 1976. Charles Caulkett (my brother) joined British Railways at Didcot in 1953, starting his career as most people did at that time, cleaning engines, later becoming a fireman. Working at Didcot and Reading after national service, Charles returned to British Rail, transferring to the southern region (including Weymouth) in 1975. After working as a passenger guard on the Wessex Trains for many years, Charles retired in 2001.

Left: Rita Jennings, who worked at Warners the chemist for twenty-five years.

Below: Egg packers' dinner dance, 1959. Pictured are: Mr and Mrs Essex, Harry and Hazel Marriot, Mr and Mrs Weston, Pete and Margaret Smith, Veronica Elsley and Don Whyte, John Cully and Richard Aldridge.

Above: First World War Photo, possibly taken in 1918. Back row third from left is George Dibden (railwayman).

Right: Mr Webb and Olive, his daughter, outside the old Pioneer Garage on the Lower Broadway, sometime in the 1940s or '50s.

G.W.R.Junction, Didcot, Berks.

Above: Didcot Station in the 1920s. Station Garage can just be seen on the left of the platform.

Left: Wagon bursting down the Dardanelle (British Rail) in the 1950s or '60s. Seated from left to right are: Eric Poole, Randell Reece and Joe Pope. Front: Len Smith.

From left to right: Eric Bellamy, Randell Reece, Sid Hawkins and Fred Wigley.

At the rear are: Eric Bellamy, Fred Wigley, - ?- (charge hand), Sandy Morrison, Roy (Nobby) Brown. Front row: Len Smith and Sid Hawkins.

At the top, seated, are: Morney Brown, Sid Hawkins, and Fred Wigley. In front is Roy (Nobby) Brown.

At the rear are: Eric Bellamy, Sid Hawkins, and Sandy Morrison. In front are Fred Wigley, -?- (charge hand), and Len Smith.

At the rear is Les Stratton. Seated are
Fred Wigley, Eric Bellamy and Joe Pope.
In front are Len Smith and Sid Hawkins.

Don Osbourne, photographer. In January
2004 my old class and school friend Don
Osbourne hung up his cameras after a
lifetime of photography. Studio Atlanta
was first started in the 1940s by Francis
Atlanta Adams. The firm was situated
in Church Street at this time, and Ted
Smith was the next photographer to take
over the helm with Don taking over
the reins in 1963. Ted later emigrated to
Australia. The business had moved to the
Broadway and later to a former butchery
in Mereland Road. Although Don has
now retired and lives in Drayton, he is
still asked to do the occasional photo for
old customers and friends.

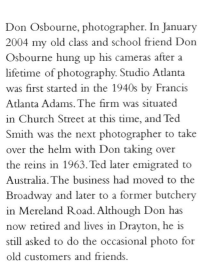

Above: Mr Alfred Carpenter, pictured, was certainly the first photographer I can remember in Didcot, although I believe a Mr Evans was taking photographs in Didcot earlier than him. Alf used his motorcycle and sidecar and worked from home until getting premises along Foxhall Road. Alf took thousands of photos during his lifetime, keeping everybody happy with his professional style. Later on, in retirement, he spent many years in the lovely village of West Hagbourne.

Opposite below: Didcot loco shed, Saturday 17 July 2004. From left to right: A. Fenn, R. Cotterall, A. Lyford, E. Watts, R. Jones, M. Davies, E. Morgan, A. Davies, G. Barnes, J. Pritchard, R. Hooper.

Right: Studio Atlanta photographer Ted Smith took over the business sometime in the 1950s. He was often helped by his younger brother Eric, who became quite an accomplished photographer in his short time with his brother Ted. Ted sold the firm to Don Osbourne in 1963 and emigrated to Australia.

Below: Photographer Caroline White stands proudly outside her shop, which she established in 1998. Caroline enjoys being based in Didcot and has made many new friends while building up a steady business. We all wish her every success in her ventures.

Above: Didcot firemen on board a fire engine in about 1921. The fire station at that time was on the junction of Wessex Road and Mereland Road.

Following many years working as a journalist on newspapers, Willie Pereira, pictured, decided to give up this line of work and return to his first love: photography. It was during his school days in his birthplace in Nairobi, Kenya, that Mr Pereira first picked up a camera and began photographing his friends, landscapes, sports and other events, as well as the odd wedding. Towards the end of his student days he decided to take part in one of Kenya's early outward bound mountain school courses, which included Kilimanjaro. Inevitably, his camera went up the mountain with him and he returned with a rich photographic record of the adventure. Soon after, Pereira joined the police in Kenya as a civilian apprentice. Some of his early photographs found their way into Kenyan and South African publications.

It was this involvement with newspapers that led him to further his studies in the UK; he took a diploma course in journalism at the then polytechnic in London's Regent Street. This was followed with reporting work until, finally, he decided to revert to photography, starting Isis Studios in Cockcroft Road in Didcot. Since then he has photographed thousands of local weddings, and has taken portraits of countless generations of families. Industrial photography was also one of his interests and many local firms were his clients.

Combining both his reporting and photographic interests, Mr Pereira published guide books for Wallingford and Didcot. His last venture in this field was co-authoring the *East Hagbourne Times*. This so-called portrait of an English village has helped raise funds for East Hagbourne projects including the relocation of the post office store, a new village hall sign, and paying for the base on which a globe, used to illustrate the ecological work undertaken by pupils, was mounted in the school grounds. One of the other projects that Pereira has been involved in was the publication of local postcards. He continues to live in Didcot.

Opposite below: Will Pryor (father of Basil Pryor) is seen here, in the third row from the front, third in from the right, wearing many medals from the First World War. Ron Andrews is also in the same row, fourth from the left. The man in the Anthony Eden-style hat is Mr James Morse, who was a parish clerk for many years. This photograph was taken outside Barclays Bank on the Broadway, which was a chemist at the time.

Above: On the pavillion at Edmonds Park, *c.* 1960. Back row, from left to right: -?-, Linda Price, Diane Carroll. Front row: Nobby Bennett, Margaret Ryan, Gillian Humphreys, Pauline Davis, Judith Pearce, Dorothy Willis.

Below: Old friends lark about at Edmonds Park. From left to right: Barry Rickard, Ken Caulkett, John McInnerny, Pete Goodenough.

Right: Barry Rickard with girlfriend Dawn Pilling, Edmonds Park, *c.* 1953–54. Dawn and Barry later married and are still happily together after forty-five years.

Below: Barn Youth Club rounders team, 1952. From left to right: Marina Birmingham, ? Langley, Beryl Smith, Robin Walters, Kathleen Osler, Jim Willis, Dave Robson, Val Bullavant, Neville Waddicor.

Left: Edmonds Park, *c.* 1954. Dawn Pilling shares a laugh with all her mates while posing for the camera.

Below: Edmonds Park, *c.* 1960. From left to right: Gillian Humphreys, Linda Price, Judith Pearce, Pauline Buckle, Pauline Davis, Dorothy Willis, Margaret Ryan, Diane Carroll. The flats in the background have now long gone.

Right: Barry Rickard and friend Alan Caulkett (Sonny), my brother, pose for a picture by the war memorial on the corner of Edmonds Park, *c.* 1955.

Below: Royal British Legion, dedication of the three standards, in the 1950s. From left to right: RASC Jack Amphlett, John Belton and Mr Lewis. The blessing took place on the pavilion in Edmonds Park.

Didcot Athletic six-a-side football team, Edmonds Park, in the late 1940s. From left to right, back row: Brian Bidemead (?), Keith Evans, Fred Balcombe. Front row: David Caswell, -?-, Ian Williamson, Reg Stokoe.

Barn Youth Club, Didcot Station onward to Avon Tyrell, 1951. From left to right, back row: Ann Richards, Mary Murray, Marina Birmingham, Arthur Hitchcock, Jim Willis, Tony Jefferies, Mick Jefferies. Middle row: Barbara Piesley, Roger Woodley, Terry Lamerton, Roly Manning, John Wilcox. Front row: Margaret Swanzy, Gill Drewitt, Bridget Swanzy, Dave Richards, Neville Waddicor, Billy Thompson.

two

Sport

Above: Didcot Athletic FC, winners of the North Berkshire League, 1959/60. Pete Gregory and Nick Nickolos are pictured.

Left: Didcot Athletic FC, club man of the year, 1960/61. Ted Dadds with Alex Salvetti, the landlord of the White Hart (now Broadways).

Above: Didcot Athletic FC, North Berkshire
League winners, 1960/61. From left to right,
standing: Brian Johnson, John Mayall, Bill Dadds,
Cyril Evans, Ray Smith, Bob Payne, Neville
Waddicor, Paddy McGuigan, Kenny Levett,
Malcolm Slade, Bert Kent, Len Franks, Cyril
Fletcher, Nobby Bennett, Denis Maggs. Seated:
Joe McCabe, Steve Smith, Spoff Wright, Pete
Gregory, Maurice Yeatman, Ted Dadds.

Right: Joe McCabe receives Didcot Athletic
FC's player of the year award from Alex Salvetti,
1960/61.

Didcot Wednesday FC, probably about 1935/6. Standing: ? Hastings, (Johnnie?) Weaver, Jack Goodall, ? Cornish, Jack Pictor, Vic Goodall, Bert Moxon, ? Greenaway, Les Hitchcock, Mr A. Howes (Manager). Sitting: ? Carter, Joe Moxon, ? Hitchcock, ? Knight, 'Titch' Goodall. Didcot Wednesday, as the name implies, provided opportunity for young men whose time off was Wednesday afternoon (early closing day) to play football. But not all were shop workers. They played, usually, in blue and white halves. This photograph was taken in front of the old mainly wooden structure which stood on the Station Road ground at the Station Road end.

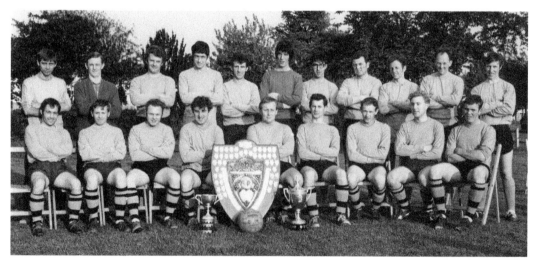

Didcot Athletic FC, winners of the North Berkshire League and Festival Cup, 1968/69. From left to right, back row: Micky (?), Eric Cann, Roger Jefferies, Norman Younghusband, Joe McCabe, Glyn Collins, Charlie Moon, Fred Cox, Norman Haycroft, Ken Haycroft, Terry O'Donovan. Front row: Pete Deakin, Neville Waddicor, Bill Cook, Danny Lloyd, Ken Gregory, ? Smith, Dave Sharp, Alan Wright, Alex Shand.

The Harwell Boys, 1952/53 runners up in the Hawkins Cup, played at Didcot Town FC. From left to right, back row: Mick Hill, ? Roberts, Don Howlett, Dick Powell, Kenny Caulkett, ? Broad, Glyn Smith. Front row: Neville Waddicor, Kenny Levett, Malcolm Mulford, Titch Green, Billy Thompson.

Didcot Rugby Club (outside the Royal Oak), 1956/57. From left to right, standing: -?-, Jim Turner, Jim Willis, Bert Buckingham (landlord of the Royal Oak), Ken Knott, Ron (Sailor) Farrell, Roy (Nobby) Brown, ? Willis, -?-, Phil Allum, ? McInnerny, -?-, -?-, -?-, -?-. Sitting: -?-, -?-, -?-, Harry Caswell, Billy Caswell, Revd Bussell, -?-, Denzil Jones, ? O'Brien.

Fleur De Lys Darts Team Cup. From left to right: Brian Burgess, Cliff Hutchings, Will Kent, Alfie Britain, Jack Parrot.

Wallingford Arms Darts Team, 1938/9. From left to right, back row: Jack Lawley, Bert Lawley, -?-, Alfred Thornhill, Mr Glover (landlord), -?-, -?-, -?-, -?-. Front row: -?-, -?-, -?-, Jack Christopher.

West Hagbourne Pigeon Club, 1973. Karen Caulkett and myself collecting the trophies from Flo Barratt (landlady).

Didcot and Hagbourne Pigeon Club presentation night, 1975. Rosemary and Graham Fry collect their trophies and certificates from Eric Barrett, landlord of the Horse and Harrow public house in West Hagbourne.

West Hagbourne Racing Pigeon Club. A new club formed a year previously from some members of Didcot pigeon club. Both clubs have now amalgamated. This photograph shows winning members in 1973. From left to right: George (Yorky) Walton, Dick Fox, Tony Mason, Flo Barratt (landlady), Terry Lamerton, Derek Jennings, Ken Caulkett, Pete McCabe. The club met at the Horse and Harrow public house, West Hagbourne.

Didcot Pigeon Club prize giving at the Civvy Hall, North Road, 1950. From left to right, front row: Titch Goodall, Eric Stovin, George Harris, Charlie Hiskins, Charles Stovin, Bill Wootton. Middle row: Jim Embling, -?-, Jock Hughes, -?-, -?-, Arthur Abbott, Mr Beechey Snr. Back row: David Hunt, George Walton, Mr Collins, Ken Beechey, Bill Wootton's brother.

West Hagbourne Pigeon Club, late 1970. From left to right: Mark Randell, Mick Randell, Graham Fry, Jim Kenny, Eamon Kelly, Frank Lloyd, Frank Morgan, Morgan Sweeney, Jean Fox, Dick Fox, Dave Hunt.

Didcot Pigeon Club prize giving, in the 1950s. From left to right, front row: (three lads): ? Lloyd, Peter Adby, Philip Adby. Middle row: Gerald Stovin, Eric Stovin, G. Harris, Ruby Goodall, Mr Hermon, Mr Cooper, -?-. Back row: Tom Butters, -?-, Titch Goodall, -?-, Frank Lloyd, David Hunt. Photograph probably taken at what they call the Nisson Hut in Cullens Field.

Presentation night at West Hagbourne Flying Club, East Hagbourne Hall, 1973. From left to right: Jill Randell, Kathy Jennings, Rosemary Fry, June Lewis, Margaret Brown (man at rear is unknown).

Didcot Rugby Club on a playing tour of France in the late 1970s. Some of those whose names I know are: Dave Hall, Steve Thomas, Pud (?), Micheal Grant (Granny), Paul Edwards, Malcolm Gillan, Mick Carol, Mack Mcgibbon, Wally Noble, Ven Sedesgy, Derek Reynolds, Mick Reynolds, Tony Grantham, Martin Llewellyn, Chung, Allan Taylor, Mick Galpin.

Didcot Youth XV, 1969/70. From left to right, back row: Peter Edwards, ? Smith, -?-, Mick Galpin, -?-, John Potter, Woody, -?-, -?-, James Careless. Front row: Tweed Hams, -?-, Bob Page, Pat Burnage, Daniel Strange, Alan Watts.

Didcot Boys: from left to right, back row: Martin Finch, Sean Oglesby, Hal Surtel, Dean McConnell, Carl Naylon, Jim Charman, Fred Balcombe (Buffy), Andy Dix, Duncan Edwards, Barry White, Kevin Hill (Berky). Front row: James Morrison, Mark Smith, Steve Hunt, Richard Lee, Paul Noble, Grange Snell.

Didcot Athletic FC, winners of the North Berkshire League Cup, 1960/61. From left to right, back row: Spoff Wright, Reg Stokoe, John Walker, Ray Smith, Bob Payne, John Slade, Nobby Bennett. Front row: Neville Waddicor, Reg Dadds, Jock Thomson, Malcolm Slade, Maurice Yeatmen.

Didcot Town. From left to right, back row: Derek Pryke, Hugh Ryan, Malcolm Jefferies, Dave Marriot, ? Gulliver, -?-. Front row: Dave Morgan, Pete Sanderson, Joe McCabe, Harry Marriot, Terry Donovan.

Didcot Athletic in the 1970s. From left to right, back row: Joe Alvey, -?-, -?-, Alan Trinder, ? Corderoy, Barry Briscoe, Alex Shand. Front row: Richard Roberts, Geoff Gough, Barry Spindler, Dennis Tyler, Brian Morris.

Six-a-side football team in the late 1940s. From left to right, back row: Percy Ball, Bill Brown, Bert Kent. Front row: Doug Robertson, Bob Butler, Gwillam Evans. It is probably the Barn Club Football Team.

Above: Didcot Athletic FC presentation dance, Majestic Hall, Reading, in 1962. From left to right, standing: Alan (Butch) Elkin, Clive Corrigan, Steve Smith, Eddie Jenks, Nobby Bennett, Bill Dadds, Terry O'Donovan, Robin Walters, Ted Dadds, Nimo Goodenough, Bob Payne, Ernie Westbrook. Crouching: Neville Waddicor, Alan Bowler, Joe McCabe, Ginger Regan, Ken Haycroft.

Left: Under 16s North Berkshire Netball Tournament, 1966. The team represented Berkshire in the south of England netball championship, held on the Isle of Wight. From left to right, back row: Kathleen Bromfield, Doreen Oglesby, Carol Ward, Jane Moon. Front row: Lyn Hetherington, Jill Nixon, Paula Barrow, Bridget Mackay.

three

The Vestas

Above: Parkside, 1949/50. Three very good friends who grew up together pose for a photo in Parkside, which is now Queensway. From left to right: Bob Kaye, Tony Poffley, Ron Caulkett.

Below: Bowness Avenue: From left to right, Bill Joslin, Don Whyte and Mike Locke.

Above left: Childhood friend John Hunt outside his home in Downs Road.

Above right: Happy times, Bowness Avenue, in the 1950s. From left to right: Sandra Young, Maureen Coles, Joan Lamerton

Right: South Park Avenue in the 1940s. With the Second World War over, Len Smith relaxes with the family. On the left is his sister Iris, and in the centre is Len's mum Iris who is holding baby Lenore, Len's daughter.

VE Day party, South Park Avenue (Nos 7 and 9 South Park Avenue are in the background). At the rear are Mr and Mrs Reynolds. Middle: Mrs Stewart, Gracie Stewart, Randell Rees, Alan Reynolds. Seated: Ann and Neville Waddicor, Ann Frewin.

VE Day party, South Park Avenue (No. 12 South Park Avenue is in the background). At the rear: Mrs Kent, Mrs Waddicor. Seated: Kent Brothers, Barbara Piesley, Ann Fewin.

The RPs rescue party, Tavistock Avenue, 1940/41. The RPs encouraged the children to wear a gas mask when needed. The young girl sees the funny side of the situation.

RP's leaving the house, rescue exercise completed, no time for a break. Most RP's had full-time jobs.

Above and below: The RPs practise their rescue operation on the Vesta Estate.

Opposite above: The Vesta Estate reunion, 26 April 2002. Dave Coles worked hard to arrange this night, a good time was had by all. Here are just some of the people who attended: Talbot, Coles, the Caulketts, Davis, the Rickards, the Baileys, Bullock, Fisher, Hewer, the Robertsons, Kent, Walton, the Dawsons, Greenaway, the Cleverleys, Target, the Randells, Tucker, the Sandersons, Burke, Thornhill, Rees, Manning, Ackerman, Roger, Hawkins, Herbert, Goodenough, Barclay, Hill, Lamerton, Nappers, Miles, Peasley, Hunt, Frewin, Waddicor, Peppin, Brooks, Stewart, Grimes, the Humphreys, Fletcher, Earls, Malloy, Robson, Woodman, Shear, Packer, Evans, Mallotti, Breeze, Harbar, James, Upham, Creswell, Nankervis, McInnerny.

Above: A Vesta Estate wedding. From left to right, back row (centre): Noni Reece, George Bullock. Middle row: -?-, Gladys Shorter, Wanda Brown, Gwen Evans, Mary Shorter, Barbara Shorter and husband, Ethel Shorter, Mrs Winnie Bullock, Vi Bailey and boyfriend Ken, and Mrs Shorter. The child standing is Freddy Shorter. The children in front are: Margaret Shorter, -?-, Vivian Viney, -?-.

Len Smith stands beside Charlie Talbot, with baby Lenore, in South Park Road. This is one of my favourite pictures as it clearly shows my childhood home, No. 23 Tavistock Avenue, on the right-hand side of the photo.

four

The
Military

Above: War Department Constabulary, 1927. From left to right, back row: Mr Jefferies (M/M), -?-, -?-, Mr Mason, Mr H. Tibble, Mr Delaney. Middle row: -?-, Mr Anderson (M/C), -?- (DCM), -?-, Mr North (Tiny), -?-, -?-, Mr Golding, -?-. Seated: Mr Harris (M/C), -?-, sergeant in the Berkshire Constabulary, chief clerk in the civil service, colonel of the ordinance depot, inspector of the WDC, -?-, -?-. Seated on the floor: -?-. The original War Department Constabulary in the Didcot Ordanance Depot, taken in 1927. All the constables were long-serving ex-soldiers, going to France in 1914 and wearing the 'P.I.P. Squeak' and Wilfred medals of the old contemptibles. All are also wearing the long service and good conduct medal and a few are wearing gallantry medals awarded during the terrible battles fought on the Western Front. All the policemen lived in married quarters in Vauxhall Barracks named the Oval. Many of their descendants still live in the Didcot area.

Opposite, top right: Sergeant Alex Robertson. He was based at times in Bowness Avenue, Didcot (his family home) during the Second World War. Bomb aimer Sergeant Robertson, like a couple of others in Didcot, would get on his bike, cycle over to Abingdon or possibly Chiltern, board a bomber and carry out one of his many missions over Europe.

Opposite, bottom right: Douglas Robertson, who served in the Royal Artillery, in 1948.

Opposite, bottom left: Henry Gladstone Abrams, R.E.M.E. He was born in a British military hospital in India, like many others in those days. At the end of school days it was time for the Army. He served in India, Palestine and also the North African campaign (in the 8th Army). He also took part in the Anzio Landings and saw action in Arnham and Italy, finishing his career in Austria after the war, having served mainly in the R.E.M.E. which was attached to many regiments.

Harold (Sam) Langford. Sam was brought up at No. 53 Parkside, Didcot – what is now the west end of Queensway. He attended the mixed-sex school at St Frideswide's, until St Birinus' was built. Sam enlisted in the Royal Berkshire Regiment at the age of seventeen years. He soon saw some action when landing on Juno Beach with this regiment on D Day. Sam was later transferred to the 2nd Battalion of Oxford and Buckinghamshire, and later he took part in the Glider Landing across the Rhine in 1945. When the war ended, Sam joined the Berkshire Constabulary and, in 1962, during his time as a village bobby at Blewbury, he rescued a man from a house fire. He was later awarded a certificate by the society for the protection of life from fire, and retired in 1976. Sam is still enjoying life, still going strong at the age of eighty-three.

Fredrick John (Jack) Butters of the Royal Navy, with wife Nancy. Fredrick was born in Sussex and he joined the HMS *Vincent* shore training base as a button boy in 1926. This was the start of a career in the Royal Navy which spanned more than thirty years. At the age of sixteen he went to sea, serving in the Mediterranean for more than two years before service in Singapore and China, where his gunboat was shelled during action between the Chinese and Japanese. Jack returned to England – via a brief spell when he was involved in the Spanish Civil War – and met Nancy, his wife to be, at Sunningdale, Berkshire, where she was in private service. The couple, who made their home in Hagbourne Road, Didcot, were married at St Luke's church, Portsmouth, in September 1939, before he embarked for South Africa. He saw active service across the world, including North Africa and the Battle of Crete in 1941, where his vessel sank and he had to be rescued after nineteen hours in the sea. Jack spent a year hospitalised with septic arthritis in North Africa before spells in Singapore and Ceylon, ferrying prisoners of war. Among his decorations was the British Empire Medal, for which he received two citations, one for helping recover a colliery ship in a storm and another for rescuing a trapped seaman.

Above left: Didcot ATS Camp, 1951. On the right is Irene Francis, who became Mrs Belton.

Above right: Len Smith spent most of the Second World War on board HMS *Cumberland*, serving his time in Singapore. He was also involved in the surrender of Java and he and his crew were responsible for the release of allied prisoners. Len also recalled the time that Lord Mountbatten received a lift to Rangoon during the surrender.

Right: Ernest Kent, who served with the 8th Army in the Middle East in the 1940s.

Above left: Thomas Waddicor.

Above right: Thomas Clifford Fedrick (Tiger), born in 1910. He arrived in Didcot from Devon in 1928 and married Eva in 1934 while serving with the RAOC at Vauxhall Barracks, and has eight children. He saw service in places including: Abyssinia, Tobruk, Palestine, Egypt, Singapore and Malaya. He retired from the army as a warrant officer in 1956, and spent some time at the Morris Motor Works in Cowley, then at the Didcot open-air swimming pool. This photo shows Tiger relaxing with his daughter Wyn in 1936.

Left: The Second World War is over, somewhere in Italy, 1945. Sergeant Charles Henry Caulkett (my father) gives the lads a laugh by showing how it's done. He served in the army for twenty-three years: nine of these were in the 9th Lancers and fourteen were spent with the Royal Army Veterinary Corps. He was a veteran of Dunkirk and saw service in Ireland, Egypt, Palestine and France, and he also took part in the Battle of Monte Casino.

five

Weddings

Miss Lenore Smith's marriage to Mr Ken Mole in 1963.

Wedding day, September 1963. Veronica and Don Whyte cut the cake at their reception in East Hagbourne Village Hall.

Right: The marriage of Nellie Faulkner and Ronald Stevenson, in 1941. Ron was serving in the Royal Berkshire Regiment at this time.

Below: The marriage of Mr Eric Smith to Miss Barbara Caulkett, 23 February 1963. From left to right: Daphne Smith (née Randell), Eileen Smith, John Long, Winifred Smith, Robin Smith, Eric Smith, Barbara Smith (née Caulkett), Ivy Caulkett, Bill Whiteman, Jean Long (née Caulkett), Carol Jones, Ron Caulkett, Sylvia Staniford (née Caulkett), Charles Caulkett, Micheal Staniford, Marion Caulkett (née Talbot), Belinda Caulkett (baby),and Alan Caulkett. The children are: Robert Smith, Steven Smith, Christine Smith, Linda Staniford, Wendy Staniford, Denise Caulkett, Vivien Smith, Anita Staniford, and Peter Staniford.

Left: The wedding of Michael Long to Dorothy Willis at St Peter's church, Northbourne. This picture was taken in 1971 at the signing of the register in the vestry. The vicar's name was Revd Edwards.

Below: The wedding of Miss Iris Smith to Mr Ray Butcher. Pictured, from left to right, are: Iris Smith, Ray Butcher, Charlie Talbot (standing behind), Iris Smith and Mr Butcher.

Above: The wedding of Mr Stephen White to Miss Diane Cox, 28 August 1997. The line-up of guests are, from left to right: Michael Axenderrie, Simon Winterbourne, Lawrence Wright, Stephen White, Carl Naylon, Charlie Caulkett, Darren Clarke. Front: Jordan Caulkett.

Below: The wedding of Mr George Goodman and Miss Eileen Peppin, 15 March 1952.

Above: Friends of Kynaston Road all line up for a photo session. They are, from left to right: Mrs Dowding, Mrs Christina Osbourne, Mr Charles (Charlie) Osbourne, Mr Tommy Faulkner and Mrs Edith Faulkner.

Left: The wedding of Cyril and Muriel Mcgibbon, at St Peter's church, 16 October 1937. Cyril served in the British Army and achieved the rank of sergeant; he was also a staunch member of the British Legion from 1945, holding various offices with the local branch. Cyril died in 1967 at the age of fifty-seven.

Opposite above: The wedding of Patricia Watts and Bert Kent, 1951. From left to right: Ines Hill, Roy Griffiths, Pat Bush, Bob Watts, Pat Watts, Bert Kent, Emmy Kent, Jean Griffiths, Ern Kent, Sheila Essex (now Dadds).

Opposite below: The wedding of Kenny Cooper. From left to right: Pete Adby, Jack Peadle, Terry Lamerton (Lammy), Brian Hoey, John Matterson, John Hoey, Henry Maddison, ? McConville, Dick Moore.

The wedding of Bob Smith and Ann Hyde at Barn church.

Above: The wedding of Bob and June Willis on the grounds of Northbourne church, 1951. From left to right: Madeline Porter, Janet Vincent, Joan Willis, Dorothy Willis.

Opposite above: The wedding of David Wharton and Caroline Byrne at Northbourne church, 25 July 1970. From left to right: Mabel Markovic, Bill Godsall, Doreen Godsall, Olive Price, –?– (baby), Maria Marovic, Jeffery Godsall, Valerie Godsall, Tracy Madge (baby), Derek Woodard, David Wharton (groom), Caroline Byrne (bride), Penny Byrne (bridesmaid), Edwina Henry (very young bridesmaid), Carol Bickell (bridesmaid), Keith Madge, Edith Faulkner, Brian Chapman, Sylvia Byrne, Tommy Faulkner, Neil Madge (young boy), Diana Madge (née Byrne).

Below: Mrs Eva Fedrick (née Lawrence) with husband Tom (Tiger), celebrating their golden wedding anniversary.

The wedding of Dave Shugar and Jean Coombs at Harwell.

six

Schools

The staff of Manor School.

The staff at Manor School relax in the grounds. This photograph was taken in the 1930s or '40s.

Class of Manor School in the early 1930s. The teacher is Miss Francis. The known children are: Nelly Faulkner, Harold Warr, Gerald Warr, Ray Crossingham, Edgar Talbot, Frank Putter, Tony Kinch, Percy Dearlove, Jean Griffiths and Jack Chamberlain.

Manor School, 1939-40. From left to right: back row: -?-, Ernie Gosford, John Bishop, Derek Creed, John Belton, -?-, -?-, -?-, -?-, John Butterfield, -?-. Middle row: Robin Strange, Cyril Huggins, Gerald Trinder, George Morris, -?-, -?-, Bill Rouse, Les Stratton, John Pryor, Harold Bennett, -?-. Front two rows: -?-, -?-, ? Walker, Reg Burnage, ?, Gordon James (behind), Reg Shaw (Titch), -?- (behind), -?-, -?- (behind), Micheal Merrett, -?- (behind), Don Walker, -?- (behind).

Headmaster James Edward Robbins watches as Cllr Les Hitchcock congratulates winners at sports day while handing out trophies.

Teams from Manor School line up for sports day in the 1950s. The sports field used by the school ran alongside Britwell Road; it is now, sadly, being eaten up by buildings.

June Queen. Country dancing display in Manor School playground in 1948.

Manor School June Queen, 1948.

Didcot Manor School May Queen with flowers. The queens are Kath and Jill Belton.

Manor School May Queen, 1946.

Manor School play, 1948.

School play, 1944. From left to right: Richard Watts, David Davis, -?-, -?-. Robert Kimber, Philip Davies (standing on chair), -?-, -?-, -?-, -?-.

June Queen, 1944. The attendants with baskets are Freda Brazier and Janet Watts. Seated is Shirley Davis (third from right).

School play, 1948. Richard Watts is first on the left.

Six girls from Manor School represent the school in the district sports events.

May Day in the 1950s. The children of Manor School celebrate May Day while Mr Robbins (the headmaster) looks on.

St Frideswide's Netball Team, 1955. Back row, from left to right: Dorothy Hardy, Jennifer Beard, Shirley Sear, Janet Sturge. Seated: Veronica Elsley, Maureen Ireson, Pauline Smith.

Mrs Lanyon Brown held a primary school in her home at No. 71 Norreys Road. She is pictured in her back garden with children, 7 November 1945. Those known in the photo are: Dorothy Wills, Marilyn Fields, Jean Saunders, Joan Tennison, John Mayall, Sheila Hayes, Jill Tappin, Maurice Yeatman, Peter Bull, Josie Sneeseby and Brian Breakspear.

Northbourne Netball Team, triple winners 1976. From left to right: Maria ?, ? Buckingham, Tracy Barnes, Louise Ridley, -?-, -?-, Maria Willoby, -?-.

Class of St Frideswide's, 1983. From left to right, back row: Emma Bowler, June Snook, Zoe Beard, Debbie ?, Sharon Wharton, Donna Nicholson, -?-, Stacey Andrews. Middle row: Mrs Holt (tutor), Anna Gibson, -?-, Glenys Walters (?), Nicola Heald, Charlotte Webb (?), Dawn Oakley, Leigh ?, Andrea Turner. Front row: -?-, Anne Smith, Rosemary Lew, Helen Hughes, Lisa Cochrane, Tara Hopkins, -?-.

St Frideswide's Secondary Modern School, 1961. This was the first secondary modern where pupils could take GCEs in the country. Front row, third from the right, is Dorothy Long (née Willis).

St Frideswide's School, 1955. Carol Cummings, Wendy Webb, Sally Neal, Norma Curry, Rosemary Leech, Maureen Ireson, Janet Tucker, Ruth Orbell, Kay Franks, Amy and Elsie Lovelock, Veronica and Angela Elsley, Jennifer Beard, Margaret Webb, Susan Tyrrol, Linda Couling, Mary Lawton, Diane Yates, Dorothy Harding, Audrey Gardiner, Pauline Levett, Maureen Bennett, Janet Sturge, Shirley Sears, Diane Carroll, Julie Philips, Pauline Davis, Mary Hobbs.

St Birinus' Football Team, 1952. From left to right, back row: Mr Robinson, John Lightfoot, -?-, Paul Kavener, Malcolm Harmer, Robert Treadwell, Graham Hodges, Mr Strong. Front row: Mr Barclay, Neville Waddicor, Billy Thompson, Ivor Bowden, Ken Polley, John Cannon, Mr Robinson.

Didcot Boys School prefect group, 1953/54. From left to right, back row: John McInnerny, David Fitchett, Alan Mayhew, Pat Burton, Billy Thompson, Keith Presland. Front Row: Dave Hearman, ? Mattocks, Brian Spindler, Mr Mulford, Albert Reed, Don Osbourne and Gordon Bartrum.

Above: Northbourne Netball Team, winners 1983. From left to right, back row: Lisa Vass, Sam Clark, Kirsty Diamond, Toni Reardon. Front row: Gail Barnes, Stephanie Mole, Nikki Breeze and Sarah Li.

Left: Northbourne Netball Team, 1983/84. From left to right, back row: Nina Ferrie, Amanda Hornblow, Mrs Mann, Amanda Brownley, Samantha Long. Front row: Joanne Hicks, Gillian Fostakew, Vicky Cheshire.

Opposite above: Children in class. Photograph taken possibly in the 1940s or '50s.

Opposite below: Class at St Frideswide's Girls School. Unfortunately, their names are unknown.

St Frideswide's School trip to Holland, upper sixth-form class, 1961. Second on the left in the front row is Dorothy Long (née Willis).

Outing by the Didcot Girl Guides. In front, far right, is Brenda Whyte.

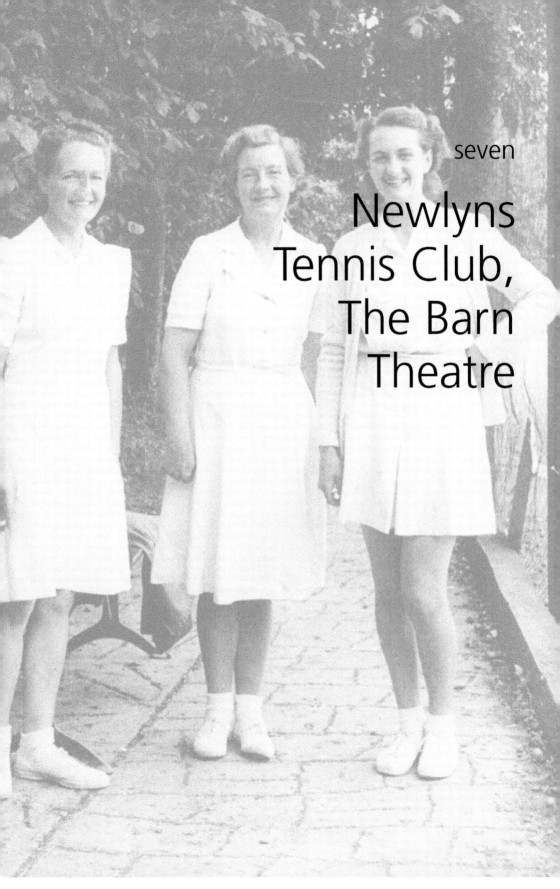

seven

Newlyns
Tennis Club,
The Barn
Theatre

Newlyn Tennis Club played on a hard court in the garden behind Smallbone Sweet Shop, on the Broadway, near the top of Haydon Road, and was owned by Mrs Smallbone and her son Leslie. The shop was previously a private house and had a long drive down to the courts and surrounding orchard. Les kept cows on the meadow at the bottom of Haydon Road (which was not tarmacked until the 1940s), and would drive them up Haydon Road to the cowsheds at the bottom of his garden to be milked. Quite often they would find their way into the garden of the Watts family at No. 27 Haydon Road, and would take a bit of moving at times.

The tennis club flourished, especially during the Second World War when there was double summer time and play went on till as late as 11.00 p.m. Babies were put to sleep in their prams under the apple trees while their mothers played tennis. A friend of mine, John Belton, who worked for Les at times, remembers pulling a large coconut mat over the court to level the surface when necessary. This information was supplied by Marion Folkes (née Watts).

Left: Ladies team, 1950. From left to right: Mrs Ruth Pepper, Mrs Kit Watts, Mrs Joan Warr.

View from window at No. 27 Haydon Road, 1941. There was no Edinburgh Drive or buildings beyond our house. Instead, there were just fields and pastures with Station Road houses, the railway line and Wittenham Clumps on the horizon.

Tennis club members, 1951. From left to right, back row: Jim Sanderson, Les Smallbone, Eric Thorman, -?-, Frank Marshall, Ken Messinden, Jack Turner, -?-. The ladies, from left to right in the centre row, are: Joan Balsam, Joan Warr, Mrs Smallbone, Joan Turner, Monica Essex. Front row: Kit Watts, Clair Watts, Bill Warr, Iris Warwick, -?-, Rhoda Sanderson. Bill Warr worked on the railway, as may have been the case with Ted Essex. Mo Essex was a teacher (at Northbourne). Rhoda Sanderson lived in Parkside (the Vestas). Mr Howes owned the grocery shop on the Broadway. Dave and Iris Warwick lived at the bottom of the Broadway near Marsh Bridge, in a bungalow with land which has now been built over. Iris ran a hairdressers shop in the Broadway.

Tennis club supper in the late 1940s. From left to right: -?-, Bill Warr (with daughter Joan on knee), -?-, -?-, -?-, Joan Balsam, -?-, Monica Essex, -?-, Jim Sanderson, Kit Watts, Clair Watts, Iris Warwick, Les Smallbone, -?-, Mrs Smallbone (mother of Les), Rhoda Sanderson, Mr Howes (?).

Men's team, 1951 (?). Back row, from left to right: Mr Howes, Dave Warwick, Les Smallbone, Ken Messinden, Jim Sanderson. Front row: Jack Turner, Clair Watts, Bill Warr.

Newlyn juniors, 1951 (?). Back row: Don Drew, -?-, Pete Sanderson, Jim Marshall. Middle row: -?- , Basher Birmingham, Pete Welch, Vince Crowley. Front row: Betty Wheeler, Pat French, Christine Sanderson, -?-, Marion Watts, Sylvia Kuhn, Joan Balsam, -?-, -?-.

While raising money to convert the old YMCA building in Park Road into a theatre, the Barn Theatre Group organised a number of dances and other events. This photograph was taken at a barn dance in the Old Coronet, 15 April 1952, and shows, from left to right: Dorothy Willis (wife of Joe), -?-, -?-, Eddie Willis, Betty Cripps, Joan Willis, June Young, Margaret Robson and Joan O'Hare.

The Barn Theatre Group. The group began its life in the old Barn church on the corner of Parkside and Park Road. By 1952, however, the members of the group had transformed the old YMCA building near the Wallingford Arms crossroads into their own theatre. The opening production was *Flowers for the Living* and both on-stage and off-stage members are shown here. Pictured are: John Nicholson, Margaret Roberts, Bill Brind (the group's director), Mildred Hubbard, Norman Roberts, June Young, Pat and Betty Cripps, Joan Willis, Sylvia Beaman, Wyn Spinks, Joyce Eggleton, John Abbott, Alan Thompson, Alan and Phil Jones, Tony Whitmarsh, Fred Cox and Reg Riley.

These pages: Over the years the group raised money for their own theatre in many different ways. One of the most popular was a series of reviews performed not only in Didcot but in many of the surrounding villages, often on dark, cold, wet nights in isolated village halls where the changing room was the field in which the hall stood. Those years forged great bonds among group members and the BTG became one of the most mutually supportive of voluntary institutions in the town. These five photographs are of reviews in the period 1950–52.

Above: The BTG produced a play a month, from September to June each year – a staggering achievement for an amateur group. Included was a pantomime which ran for a week in the post-Christmas season. The 'orchestra' for these productions was Joan Willis at the piano, who was later joined by 'Chick' Fowler with his keyboard. This picture is of the cast of *Snow White*, produced at the end of 1953 and early 1954.

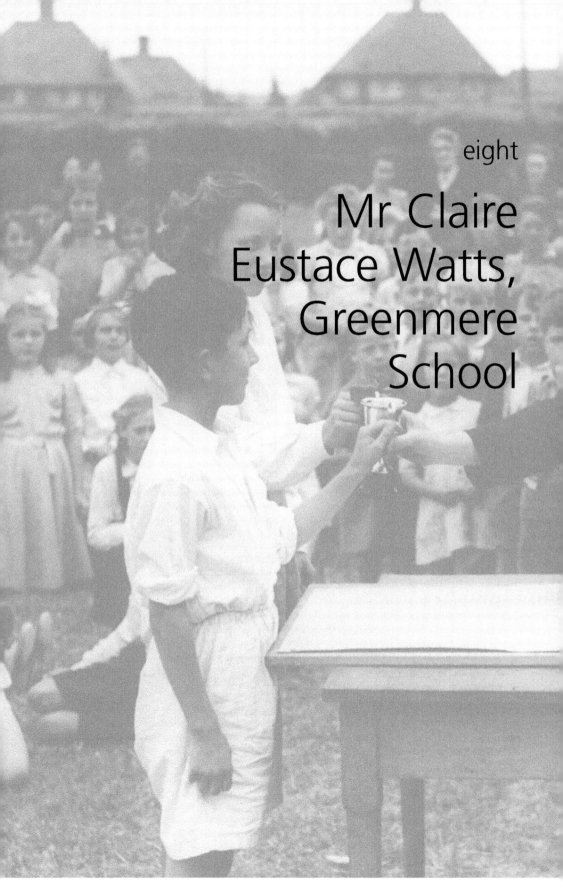

eight

Mr Claire Eustace Watts, Greenmere School

What follows is a short history of C.E.C. Watts (headmaster of Greenmere School). Clair Eustace Charles Watts was born in Cairo in the year 1901. His father was Warrant-Officer Fredrick Charles Watts of the Seaforth Highlanders and his mother was the headmistress of an army school. Understandably, he inherited from his soldier-father an uprightness, not only of bearing but of character also, and from his mother not merely a love of learning but the desire to pass it on. Throughout his life music stood high in his esteem and he always endeavoured to instill a love for it in his pupils, with great success.

Soldiers of the 1900s never settled long in one place and in 1903 his father W.O. Watts was transferred to the cooler climate of Fort George in Scotland. After a short stay, it was the fair city of Dublin, Ireland for the Watts family. Bermuda was the next stop and it was here that Clair Watts started lessons in the Army school under the watchful eye of the very strict but kind headmistress. With his father's tour of duty over, the Watts family headed home to England and for the second time in his young childhood Clair Watts and family survived a really nasty storm at sea. This time was posted overdue by Lloyds.

With the start of the First World War and the family based at Aldershot, Clair Watts attended Alton Grammer School. When the war and his time at Alton was over, it was the Duke of York's Military School in Dover for Clair, where he trained to be an army school master. After completing three years of training, he returned to Aldershot and became headmaster of Longmoor Army School.

Having had enough of army life and its limited area of teaching, Clair Watts became a civvy and in 1924 became assistant headmaster at Polehampton Boys School in Twyford. The headmaster at the time was A.S.B. Minhinnick, who would later leave his mark on Didcot, both in and out of school. At the time, Clair was still not entitled to full pay, so for a second time he took a course at a training college. When the training was completed, Clair obtained a residential post at a Home Office school for Jewish boys in Hayes, Middlesex. What he didn't know was that most of them were what we now call juvenile delinquents, and knife fights were frequent. Not happy with this, Clair made his way to Berkshire, taking on the position of assistant master at Pangbourne, where one of his pupils was none other than the later-to-be Didcot teacher Mr C.S. Page.

It was also here that Clair met another teacher, Kathleen Wood, who would later become Mrs Watts. In 1929 he became headmaster of Sonning Boys School where he put in endless work, at one time teaching night school at Twyford and Pangbourne to make ends meet. In 1936 a new infant school was opened in Didcot, the first of its kind in Berkshire. From ten applicants, C.E.C. Watts was chosen as its first headmaster; oddly enough, his successor at Sonning was S. Aubrey, who later became headmaster of Manor School.

Clair's task of establishing a new school was enormous, and most of the children attending belonged to families who had recently moved to Didcot. Many were from London and Wales, and some were poorly fed and clothed. The depots at Didcot and Milton gave most of them work, but Clair Watts often dug deep into his own pocket to help many children. In 1944, while recovering from a serious illness at Wingfield Hospital Oxford, I received a large box of biscuits from him which were hard to come by during the Second World War.

School dinners in the war were available, but the job of collecting the provisions fell to the headmaster, who did so on his bike. Mr Watts was also a captain in the Army Cadet Force when free of his ARP duties. With the war over his family life became complete: Janet was born just before the war and Marion and Richard were born during the it.

The school in the late forties was bursting at the seams with pupils, and 1950 saw the opening of the present Greenmere School, with Watts as headmaster. He continued his devotion to the school and everybody concerned with it until finally retiring in 1966. Mr Clair Watts throughout life put everything into helping others and possibly wore himself out. He sadly died in 1968 in the old Radcliffe Hospital. Mrs Kathleen Watts moved to Norwich where she died in 1989, after living for forty years in Didcot.

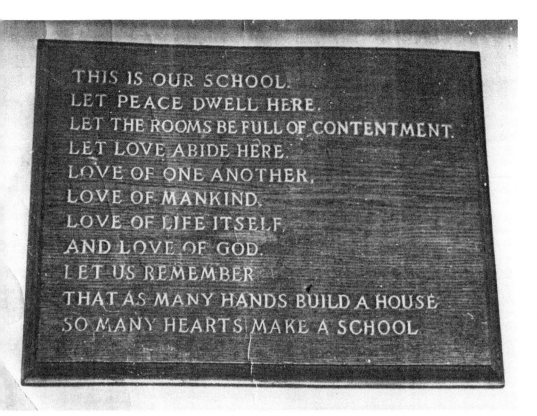

Greenmere School prayer.

The building of Greenmere School, 1936.

Greenmere School staff, 1945. Second from the left in the back row is Mrs Smith. In the centre are Mrs Payne and Mr Watts.

Above: Greenmere School staff, 1938. Mr Watts is in the centre.

Opposite above: Greenmere School staff, 1949. From left to right, back row: Mr Malcolm, Miss Payne, Mr David Calvin-Thomas, –?–, –?–, –?–. Front row: –?–, Miss Latham, Mr Watts, Mrs Smith, Mrs Lee.

Opposite below: Greenmere School staff in the 1950s. From left to right, back row: –?–, Mrs Lee, Mr Malcolm, Miss Payne, –?–, –?–, Mr Rigby. Front row: Mrs Thomas (?), –?–, Mr Watts, Mrs Smith, Mrs Watts.

Left: Greenmere School Running Team, 1953. From left to right, back row: Barbara Herman, Jane Carter. Front row: Maureen Coles, Veronica Elsley.

Below: Prize giving at sports day with Mr Watts. The photo was taken in the 1950s.

Opposite above: School visit to Paignton, 1951. Pupils are with Mrs Smith, Mr Watts and Mr Thomas.

Opposite below: A week's holiday in Paignton, Devon for Greenmere School in 1953. The teacher is Mr Rigby.

Greenmere School holiday to Paignton, 1953. In front is Veronica Elsley while at the back are: Pauline Davis, Michael Jennings, Brian Mills and the Hodge twins.

Greenmere School activities. By the 1950s it was possible to take children out on day trips (on Tappins' Coaches) for educational visits. By the mid-1950s Mr Watts began one-week educational visits to Devon, staying at Maidencombe or the Hotel Bonais in Paignton. Several pupils had never been out of Didcot before, let alone seen the sea. The teachers are Mr Watts, Mrs Lee and -?-. The photo was taken in around 1954 in Devon; amongst the pupils is Christine Piossel.

School visit to Southampton. Pictured are Mr Watts, Mrs Smith and pupils.

A tour of the Moors with Mr Watts, Mrs Watts and Marion Watts.

Greenmere School, Didcot, 1962/63. Sixth from the left in the back row is Robert Farrell; Lindy Bygraves is second from the right in this row. The middle row's names are unknown. In the front row are: Paul Kelly, Kevin Butler, Alan Pratt, Gary Fisher, Anne Lovelock, Denise Price, Andrew Lane, Pauline Dawson, -?-, -?-, John Wells, Lesley Bailey and Steve Caulkett.

Greenmere School, Didcot, 1964/65. From left to right, front row: -?-, -?-, -?-, Kevin Jones, Colin Slinn, Tony Purvis, -?-, Robin Claridge, -?-. Second row: -?-, Valerie Wells, Janet Street, -?-, Mrs Quinnell (teacher), -?-, Sheila Fisher, Karen Caulkett, Jackie Ireson. Andrew Smith is sixth from the right in the third row. Back row: -?-, -?-, Marie Purvis, Paula Noble, Maria Mandrake, -?-, -?-, -?-. Other pupils at the time include: Kim Kelly, Yolanta Klonosky, Micheal Sergeant, Wayne Bryan, Carol Chapman, Andy Beard, John Lovelock, Annette Sear, Yvonne Northover, Kim Fedrick, Susan Gibson, Susan Swanborough, Elaine Jones, Joy Beard, Marion Hughes, Steve Carter, Paul Morris, Susan Gayley, Sandra Turner and Marion Tye.

Greenmere School Football Team, 1963/64. From left to right, back row: ? Pierce, Peter Jaremchuk, David Barlow, –?–, –?–, –?–, Alan Brown. Front row: –?–, –?–, Jamie Evans, Alan Watts, –?–.

Class of Greenmere School. From left to right, front row: Paula Duke, David Williams, Mandy Jennings, Michael Root, Shane Burgoyne, Maxim Walters, Andrew Major, Alice Kerrigan. Second row: Mr Crane (teacher), Rachael Stone, Alex Hancock, Susanna Hill, Adrian Wilkins, Tracy Collins, Daniel Ryan, Sarah Jones, Steven West. Third row: Samantha Jones, Philip Kent, Hayley Pitson, Stephen ? , Christopher Shaw, Richard Wright. Back row: Dave Slade, Jago Morris, Liane Wharton, Sarah Wicks, Paul Gower, Nicola Moss.

Left: Mr Watts with the head boy and head girl (both unknown). The photo was taken in the late 1950s.

Below: Wartime officers of the Army Cadet Force in the 1940s. Second from the left in the front row is Mr Watts (headmaster of Greenmere School). Fourth from the left in the same row is Mr Jimmy Robbins (headmaster of Manor School).

nine

People of Didcot

The Willis family. From left to right, back row: Jim, Geoff. Centre: Dorothy, Bob, Joe, Eddie, Joan. In front are proud parents George and Gladys.

The Gardener family stand for a photo outside the home of Mr and Mrs Gardener in Wessex Road. From left to right: Betty Gardener, ? Gardener, Tom Gardener, Bob Gardener, Ern Gardener, Flo Gardener, ? (young girl), Fred Barnes, Jean Gardener, Brian Gardener, Ann Gardener, June Gardener (née Faulkner) with baby, ? Gardener and Ron Gardener.

Cyril and Edith Moxon on the occasion of their golden wedding in 1960. At that time they lived on the Abingdon Road in a bungalow which has long since been demolished. They are pictured with their family.

Mrs Edith Elsley celebrates her seventy-fifth birthday. She is celebrating in the presence of her daughters: Rosalind Moor, Maureen Bowl, Christine Hillman, Joy Fox, Edith Elsley (mum), Angela Fensoms, Veronica Whyte and Theresa Varley.

The McGibbon family. This photo was taken in 1955 at the British Legion Christmas party, at the Territorial Army hut in Newlands Avenue. In the top left of the picture is Nurse Watson, a resident of Wessex Road who, when needed, delivered most of the McGibbons. The children are, from left to right: Richard, Diane, Sue, Muriel, Philip and Willie.

Outside Northbourne church in 1993, the McGibbons are grown up. From left to right: Sue, Philip, Richard, Willie, Diane, Bob, Maureen and Arthur.

Neville Webb with his daughter Jackie enjoying the day at an unknown wedding reception.

The Old Police Club in the 1950s. Friends and relatives are enjoying a quiet evening out at the Old Police Club at Didcot Barracks. From left to right: Maryse Abrams, Mr Smith, Gordon (?) Smith, Percy Abrams Snr, Louisa Abrams, Henry Abrams Jnr (standing), Edna (Betty) Abrams and Patricia Abrams.

A celebration of the life of Helen Grant, in the civic hall, 2002. From left to right: Carol Crook (née James), Helen Grant (née Smith) (1967 to 2003), Barbara Smith (née Caulkett).

Mrs Myra Dowding on the occasion of her 104th birthday at the Kingswell restaurant in September 2005.

Didcot Methodist church, Wesley Guild (taken not later than 1955). From left to right, back row: Joe Bell, John Mitchell, Nurse Stacy, Nurse McNeil, Norman Curry, James Morse, Mr Carpenter, Stella Rowland. Second row: Mrs Goudge, Margaret Lee (behind), Mrs Henderson, John Henderson (behind), Mrs Ireson, Gwen Jeremy, Sylvia Deacon, Jim Jeremy, Elsie Bowler, Ken Bowler, Maud Cox, Mrs Beard, Alan Jeremy. Front row: Sergeant Perry, Mrs Carpenter, Bert Rowland, Revd George Thompson Brake, Mr Latham, Godwyn Bradbury, Mrs Carter, Mrs Timms and Mrs Hicks.

Amongst the popular events at Didcot Methodist church, especially during and immediately after the Second World War, was the annual 'Women's Weekend'. This always included a concert on the Saturday night and Sunday services led by women of the church. This photograph from the late 1940s shows: Mrs Adlam, Mrs Rowland, Mrs Rose Smith (wife of the then minister), Mrs Goudge, Mrs Cox, Mrs Bowler, Mrs Lothian, Mrs E. Moxon and Miss Mildenhall.

A dance in the Old Coronet Ballroom in 1951, probably organised by the Barn Theatre Group. From left to right, standing at the back, are: Vince Crowley, -?-, John Sweetzer. Sitting: Molly ?, Pat Cripps, Joan Willis, Sally Witney, Margaret Roberts, Mrs Cripps.

Dance at the Didcot Coronet Ballroom in 1950.

Victory party at the camp in Vauxhall Barracks in 1945.

Dance at the Garrison Theatre in the 1950s.

Above: Presentation to Mr Anderson the postmaster, in around 1955. Those pictured include: Dorothy Wills, Alan Roberts, George Wooton, Alan Back, Billy O'Reilly, Reg Harris, ? Uzmar, Joe Henderson, ? Pease, Alf Stevens, Mr Anderson, Viv Jenkins, Mrs Harris, ? Tyrell, Karen Freer and Joan Balsam.

Didcot Methodist church Women's Weekend, around the early 1950s. Pictured, from left to right, are: May Adlam, Yvonne Goudge, Mrs Goudge, Mrs Case, Mrs Hicks, Grace Smith, Mrs Greenough, Mrs Radway, Mrs Longstaffe, Mrs Carter, Stella Rowland, Mrs Warwick, Mrs Timms, Maud Cox, -?-, Ruby Moxon, -?-, Mrs Gifford, Edith Moxon. The two girls in front are Ann Moxon and Maureen ?.

Above: Children in fancy dress and their parents at the Coronation street party on Ridgeway Road in 1952. Sixth and seventh from the left in the back row are Mr Watts and Revd Pat Keating.

Opposite below: Army cadets – Newlands Avenue cadet huts, around Christmas, 1959. From left to right, back row: Tim O'Rourke, -?-, Bernard Smith, -?-, Tommy Cuddon, Kenny Cooper, -?-, -?-, -?-. Middle row: Peter Joslin, Micheal Boik, Ginger Kelly, -?-, Lieutenant McGill, ? Kernsley, -?-, Neil Mitchell, -?-, -?-. Front row: ? Dawson, John Miller, Paul Greetham, -?-, Ray Hill, Jack Peedle.

Above: Lina Beer holding Richard Amphlett, with brother Brian seated next to them. This photo was taken the day after the aeroplane crash in Cow Lane, which dates it around 22 April 1944. In the background people can be seen looking at the crash. Lina lived next door to the Amphletts in Kynaston Road from about 1936 and worked at the Co-op stores on the Broadway, whose manager, I think, was a Mr Deadman. During the war she was held in Holloway Prison for a time following malicious gossip by a neighbour involving the fact that she was a German married to a British soldier before the Second World War. A petition was organised by Fred Amphlett and presented to the high court at the Old Bailey, after which she was released. She returned to Germany in 1947.

A good night was had by all. Pictured are pals Colin Campbell, Willie Grimes and Mick Mills. This photograph was taken in the late 1970s.

Above: Richard Kelly (Dick) warms up for the night's entertainment. Dick toured many local pubs and clubs with his old pal Dave Major. This photograph taken in around the late 1960s

Opposite below: Old folks' Christmas party at the Conservative Club. From left to right, back row: Mrs Amphlett, Jack Slade, Mrs Slade, Jack Pictor, Kathy Jones, Eileen Pictor, Connie Davis, Lucy Greenaway. Front row: Gladys Well's father, Mrs Daniels (?), Florence ?, -?-, Jack Doyle, Marjorie Doyle, Mrs Smith, Mrs Freeman, -?-, Mrs Bennett.

Venue unknown, 1960. From left to right: Mike Newman, Dave Shugar, Neville Waddicor, Peggy Newman, John Shepherd, Joan Levett.

All Saints' Youth Club, 1960. From left to right: the Jessamay brothers, Sam Bosley, Jamie Coates, Tony Sturt, Ken Levett, Dave Davis, Dave Shugar, Mike Ashmore, Mike Newman, Neville Waddicor and ? Kimber.

Opposite above: Didcot Methodist Choir in around 1958. From left to right, back row: Revd Guy Stanford, Stella Rowland, Sally Carter, Bill Smith, Mr Jones, Mr Lemmon, Alec Chenery. Front row: Doug Parker, Edith Moxon, Joy Neale, Mrs Case, Maud Cox, Mrs Nash, Mrs Henderson.

Above: Didcot Methodist church Wesley guild Christmas party in around the early 1950s. From left to right, back row: –?–, Margaret Lee, Norman Curry, John Mitchell, Mrs Brake, John Rowland, Sylvia Deacon, Yvonne Goudge, Stella Rowland, Felix Goudge. Second row (standing): Grace Smith, Mrs Ireson, ? Aldridge, Mrs Bourne, Gwen Jeremy, Mrs Gardner, Joan Aldridge, Mrs Carpenter, Mrs Perry, Edith Moxon, Mrs Adlam, Mrs Goudge, Sergeant Perry, Mrs Timms, Mrs Beard (?). Front row (sitting): Nurse Stacy, Mrs Eldridge, Nurse McNeil, Mrs Hicks, Mrs Warwick, Mrs Carter, Maud Cox. Sitting on the floor: Bert Rowland, Mr Carpenter, David Jeremy, Beryl Mayhew.

Barn Youth Club, Avon Tyrell, in 1951. From left to right, back row: Tony Woodman, Terry Lamerton, Billy Thompson, Roger Woodley, Guy Stovin, Jim Willis, John Wilcox, Michaell Jefferies, Jack Reeve. Middle row: Dave Richards, Tony Jefferies, Mary Murray, Arthur Hitchcock, Marina Birmingham, Neville Waddicor, George Wooten. Front row: Margaret Swanzy, Barbara Piesley, Gill Drewitt, Dawn Pilling, Bridget Swanzy and Ann Richards.

A day trip to Southsea. From left to right: Alan Chapman (Tiny), Angelo Granito, Dave Dawson, Dick Moore, John Matterson, Fred Barham, Trevor Coles, John Hoey and Dave Barham.

Andy Webb of Andy's Hair Fashions enjoys a night out with his good friend Paul Lovelock.

Dog show in the 1980s. Pat Abrams shows her golden retriever Katie to the judge. The civic hall is in the background.

Above left: Photo from the 1950s of, from left to right: Ron Johns, Ron Gardener and Ray Yates.

Above right: Clive Eatwell has a laugh with Harry Mills. This photo was taken in the 1950s.

Left: Everybody's friend Neville Webb poses with his pal Pip Lyford. Neville spent many years cutting hair while sharing a good joke and yarn at his shop at Cockcroft in Didcot. This photograph was taken in the early 1950s.

Above left: All Saints' church féte, 1952. Reg Hayes was
an active member of the allotments. A memorial bench
to him can be found in the Wantage Road Allotments.
Those known on the photo include: Reg Herman,
Billie Cioah, Reg Hayes and Mrs Eggleton.

Above right: Cynthia Smith proudly holds daughter
Lenore.

Right: George and Lucy Greenaway.

Other local titles published by The History Press

Haunted Oxford

ROB WALTERS

From heart-stopping accounts of apparitions and manifestations to first-hand encounters with ghouls and spirits, this collection contains both new and well-known spooky tales from around the historic city of Oxford. From spirits who haunt the libraries at the Oxford colleges and shades that sup at watering holes around the city to spectral monks and even royal ghosts, this phenomenal gathering of ghostly goings on is bound to captivate anyone interested in the supernatural history of the area.

0 7524 3925 1

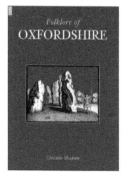

Folklore of Oxford

CHRISTINE BLOXHAM

This illustrated study of folklore rediscovers those traditions that have vanished, been ignored or hidden away, such as the lore relating to the Rollright stones and Wayland's Smithy. There are tales of poaching and highwaymen, but always at the heart of Oxfordshire's folklore are the traditional beliefs, stories, events and customs of the common people. Folklore of Oxfordshire will delight all those who wish to revel in the delights of times past.

0 7524 3664 3

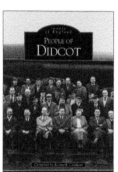

People of Didcot

KENNETH CAULKETT

This endearing collection of more than 190 photographs illustrates the history of Didcot in the early middle part of the twentieth century. The reader will encounter many faces, some known and some unknown but all who have participated in making Didcot what it is today. From the history of the Barn church and the community activities that were associated with it to the many social and sporting events that took place, this collection provides a glimpse of the people of Didcot at work and at leisure.

0 7524 2059 3

Wantage Looking Back

IRENE HANCOCK

This volume of old photographs explores the recent history of Wantage. All aspects of life are explored: from activities in the centre of the town – the Market Place – which has changed over the years yet still retains much of its original charm, to the buildings, shops, businesses and people who have come and gone to make Wantage what it is today. This book will delight those who have ever lived in or visited Wantage.

0 7524 2938 8

If you are interested in purchasing other books published by The History Press, or in case you have difficulty finding any of our books in your local bookshop, you can also place orders directly through our website
www.thehistorypress.co.uk